Chapter 1 The Beginning
Starting A Small Business
The Dream Of Many People

Starting a small business is the dream of many people. However, to make that dream a reality, it's important to understand what it takes to make it happen. There is a lot more to it than you may think, but it's not so difficult that it cannot be done.

You need to be truthful with yourself when thinking about starting a business. Are you able to motivate yourself if you don't have a boss to answer to? Are you willing to work more hours than you ever did at a job? How will you come up with the money to get started? How much will you need? What type of business will you start? Why? Do enough people need what you're offering to keep you profitable? And these are only a few of the questions you must answer.

Those may be tough questions but answering them is worth it because it means you are on your way to fulfilling your entrepreneurial dream. But why go through the hassle? The truth is that most people never will. They will run back to the comfort of the known--their job--as soon as they encounter anything that even remotely resembles an obstacle.

Don't get me wrong, there are real obstacles, and real risk, but how you handle them will determine how successful you are. Small business owners aren't special in that they get lucky or that nothing bad ever affects their business. They are special because of the way think and approach the problems when they do come up.

Starting a small business takes planning. You will need to have an in-depth plan, but it doesn't need to be perfect. The best you can do is plan based on your present knowledge of the business you would like to start. But what you know now may be quite different from the way things really are. For that reason, it's okay to change some parts of your plan. However, you shouldn't make changes lightly, and you should always have a good reason for doing so.

There are a lot of rewards that go along with having a small business. You will be your own boss, so you get to decide what you do, when you do it, and how it will be done. You will be able as much money as the market says your business is worth; no need to beg your boss for a raise. You set your own schedule, so if you want to get up at 11:00 in the morning or take a week off, then go for it! Those rewards are very real, but...

You must get to the point of running a successful small business first. You also need to be sure your business is functioning well if you want to get up late or take a few days off. But it can be done! It's going to take some effort to get to that point, but it will be more than worth it when you make your dream a reality.

Starting a small business – practical methods

Let's talk a little about what a small business is and some of the steps you will need to take to start your own.

Small business is a phrase that is used every day by millions of people across the globe. This is because during the past decade the rise of small business has become more substantial than in any other decade prior. This is largely due to the growing number of services that are offered to small business owners, to make it possible for them to keep their business running.

There really aren't any guidelines for when the term small business is used, however it is simply defined as a business which has a small number of employees. How few employees is debatable, and the definition of when a business changes from a small business to a bigger business differs both by country as well as industry. This number is generally less than 100 employees.

As I've already explained small businesses due to their nature, are usually sole proprietorships, partnerships, or privately owned. Common in many countries, smaller businesses, tend to be related to accountants, restaurants, guest houses, photographers, small shops, hairdressers, tradesmen, solicitors, lawyers, small- scale manufacturing etc.

Small businesses are often located in private homes, for two main reasons. The first is because it is cost-effective and, in most cases, convenient. The second reason is that there are several benefits with taxes, etc. by having your business in your home.

Running a small business is an exciting opportunity, a great way to introduce yourself into the business world, and to gain business sense.

But, before you spend a lot of money on your small business it's important that you know the facts, so take some time, go to the library, or get on the internet and research the basics. If possible, talk to a few experts or other small business owners so that you can be sure that entrepreneurship is right for you.

Here is a quick list of some things that you can do to get started

1. **Conduct a feasibility study of your business idea**

Describe what your typical customer, your product, and your competitors. Who will your suppliers be? What will you charge for your product? How will you market your product? These are just a few of the questions you need to answer.

2. **Write a complete business plan**

Do this using the information you gathered from your feasibility study. This is vitally important and often an overlooked step that needs to include a description of your company, its goals, competitors, market, financial information, and of course, how you intend to meet your goals.

3. **Get your financing in place**

There are many ways to finance your business, from your own savings to personal credit cards to bank loans. If you need credit, know your business plan from front to back and maybe even sideways.

4. **Decide what kind of structure your company will have**

From a legal standpoint, there are three basic choices, sole proprietorship, partnership, and incorporation, each with advantages and disadvantages.

Choose a name for your company and check on name availability

Naming your company is highly individual, but it's the first thing associated with your business, so choose your name carefully. You'll need to do a NUANS (Newly Upgraded Automated Name Search) report, which checks your name choices for uniqueness against a database of other business names. A reserved name is valid for 90 days.

Determine whether there are special permits or licenses that your business will need. Check with county courthouse or your local tax collector's office for the proper forms.

Set up your business bank account and record-keeping system

Your banker will need to see your business documents, and you may want to set up more than one account so you can keep track of your finances better. Record-keeping is required and can be done manually or with a computer program.

Purchase insurance

There are many different types of insurance, but most probably your company will need at least one. For example, if you're going to have employees, you need to have workers compensation insurance.

Decide where your business will be located

Lease your business' space. Alternatively, you could choose to start your business from home if it's feasible. There are advantages and disadvantages to starting your business from home. You have tax write-offs for example, but sometimes your image suffers.

Purchase supplies and office equipment

You'll need too many things to list here, and of course, each business has different needs. You might need a fax machine and printer. You'll probably need a computer. You'll need paper, pens, pencils and a calculator.

Being armed with the facts and information you need from the beginning is a giant step towards ensuring the success of your small business. So, take your time and do your research.

You can have a successful small business

Owning and maintaining a very successful small business can have its challenges but if you know what you are doing, everything can really work out great for you. There are many helpful tips that you should learn, if you are the owner of a small business and then by learning about these tips you should have the ability to have a very secure and profitable future.

Knowing how to operate a small business properly will give you and your employees much relief in knowing that their positions are stable and secured. Your employees will be much happier, as will you, if you do all the right things and play your cards right. In this article I am hoping to teach you a little bit more about managing a small business so that you will be a success. Having a small business has its own advantages and some of those will be included throughout this article.

It is very important for you to learn more about what it takes to run a small business successfully so that if you or someone you know becomes interested in opening your own small business, you will be much more knowledgeable about all aspects of it. Another great thing about owning your own small business is that usually this means you will for sure have many more awesome customers that will tell others about it and continue coming back themselves. You will have a reputation for owning and managing a very reputable, friendly, and affordable, yet small business.

A small business would typically go over very well because there will be enough customers to continue keeping you with plenty of customers and when people are on vacation in your area, they too have probably already heard about your small business and many of them will choose to come into your small business and will be quite pleased by the friendly employees and the great prices. Check out the other small businesses in your area to see what it is they are doing to draw in more new customers, do not copy them but kind of take a few little suggestions and ideas from watching others with more experience.

Advertising is something that most businesses do, which you as a small business owner will as well at some point in time, however, even without the professional advertising, your small business will still be successful due to all of your loyal customers that absolutely adore coming into your wonderful store. All it takes to have a very successful small business is friendliness, determination, customers that count on you and a good knowledge about business management will always make for a better chance at success.

A small business could typically go over very successfully, if you first do some homework over managing your own business, as well as talking with other small business owners because the more experienced people could really provide you with a great deal of helpful information and some tips that can almost guarantee your small businesses success and longevity.

You may have a successful business idea

You surely know that a small idea can lead to a great business success. The first movement is to think of an idea that would be suitable for the business market. After coming up with the idea, the next step is to put that idea into action. Of course, this is a very difficult step and having the idea is only the start of the journey. After that you will have to face many obstacles before being able to carry on with your business project. This is just the beginning of this process and there is a lot of questions you will have to answer before even start.

Some of the main aspects you must concentrate on when you have business ideas are the abilities and gifts you can pour into the business. It is very important for you to be identified with your business project. Those ideas should be based on activities and actions you take pleasure in doing. For example, if we suppose that you dislike working in the open, landscaping business would not suit you.

On the other hand, if you like working with children, setting up baby-sitting or tutoring business would be an excellent idea. In this case, without any doubt your business will be more successful because you will have put your mind, effort and your heart on it.

Another vital step is to analyze the needs of a specific product or service in your region before setting up your business. Do people of your area need your product? Is there other business like the one you are planning to start? You should ask yourself whether you are the only one offering that service or product. If you are not, you will have to analyze the competence you will have to face. You must think whether the service you are offering is one that customer would repeat, or if it is a one-time specialized service. Obviously, the former is more likely to succeed than the latter.

There are other aspects you must consider. These aspects are described below:

1. One of them is that if the idea is unique, you will reign the market. But if there is much competition, it will be difficult to enter the market.

2. A second point would be if you can offer quality from the very beginning, otherwise, you won't succeed.

3. Finally, you must think about your capital to start your own business. There are many business ideas that require little investment and bring great profit. Some demand research, such as daycare service, and others need a large amount of money to begin the business. So, take this recommendation into account before investing all your money in a small business idea.

How do I value my small business?

The problem with selling any small business ($500,000 and below) is how can a realistic value be put on the business. If a business is valued too high no one will be interested or worse value, it too low prospective buyers will think there is something irregular. Also, where it is listed for sale is important, EBay is a tremendous medium for certain things however fraud is commonplace.

Unfortunately, there is no fixed system when it comes to valuing any private business, the IRS, Courts of Law, and the Inland Revenue all use their own systems. There are also many wonderful mathematical formulas that can be used; however, there is no fixed system. To be honest the whole system is complicated with no fixed rule apart from one. What price is a person is happy to sell a business for and what is the buyer happy to pay?

If you are either buying or selling a small business do not be afraid of negotiation, it is a natural process within business. The following list is a simple aid to assist people who are interested in finding a value of a business, either for the sale or purchase.

1. Does the business have employees either full time or part time? Prospective buyers should be aware that any business in the UK which employs 5 or more people has specific duties regarding Health & Safety.

2. Is the business purely an internet business? Be warned it is very easy for an online business to appear to be doing very well when the truth is completely the opposite. This practice unfortunately is leading to the devaluation of genuine online businesses.

3. Does the business have fixed assets or stock? It is much easier to value a garage where real estate and equipment can easily be valued, whereas it is less easy to value a business with no fixed assets i.e., Legal specialists, Solicitors, Health workers etc.

4. Does the business have a full audit trail; it is surprising how many small businesses listed for sale do not.

5. What area is the business in; it goes without saying that businesses located closer to major cities are valued higher than businesses in a rural district.

6. What are the future growth prospects for the business?

7. Will the business require insurance/liability policies?

These are just a few factors that must be considered, as you can see there is much more to take into account than how much revenue is generated by the business. I hope this short article has been of some assistance to any potential buyer or seller of any small business.

How to get about starting

People toy with the idea of starting a small business at various stages of their lives. Some think of starting a small business after their educational career is over. Some think of starting a small business because of unpleasant or unhappy situations they have encountered in their workplaces. There are also others who think of starting a small business, because that is the only way they will be able to work again following a break from work for reasons such as health or redundancy.

Toying with the idea is one thing, but if you are taking positive steps to get started, then certain myths associated with starting and running a small business should be dispelled from your mind.

1. Starting a small business might appear to be an easy option to many who are desperate to get out of a situation but running a business is not as easy as it appears to be.

2. The general impression created in the minds of many people is that you can make a lot of money by running a small business. A few people do make a lot of money by running a small business. On the other hand, there are many people

who lose a lot of money unfortunately due to lack of proper research and planning?

3. Another myth is that you are the Boss, so you can work when you want, relax when you want and go on holidays when you want. You are the Boss that is all to it. The rest simply does not happen because of other factors that come into play which will need your presence and attention most of the time.

One major blunder made by many small business entrepreneurs is that they never made any self-assessment before starting. It is important that you do a self-assessment to find out whether you possess the following qualities and capabilities that are necessary to operate a successful small business.

1. You must be of sound health.

2. You should be able to work on your own most of the time.

3. You should be self-motivated and dedicated.

4. You should possess an outgoing personality and can get along with other people.

5. You should have the ability to work under pressure.

6. You should preferably have some knowledge about your business.

7. Failure is no option to you.

In addition to the above the following factors have a very important and significant impact in the success of your small business.

1. A good support system such as your spouse or members of your family.

2. Contacts in the business world who could help you with advice and help you promote your small business.

3. Good financial assets to help you start and develop your small business and sustain you during the early months.

Since they are popularly known as small businesses, many would be entrepreneurs are under the impression that it could be run in a slip shod manner. Most of the inputs necessary to operate a large business successfully are also necessary in the small business venture too.

Success does not come overnight. There could be disappointments and failures during the early months. Those who cannot withstand these pressures should not contemplate starting a small business. The ability to withstand all these pressures and remain motivated is necessary to succeed.

Home based small business

If you are serious about the idea of making money through home-based business, then here are tips which are a beneficial tool for those who want to begin to work at home-based business. A simple solution is to start with a business from home focused on the internet arena i.e., where the work is based on Internet.

The market is teeming with numerous ideas of home-based internet business launched by innumerable companies. Every single day new schemes come into the market under the garb of legitimate home-based internet businesses. Sadly, most of these so-called top home internet businesses are pure pyramid scams.

Home based internet businesses can be a good opportunity provided you are serious about it. With increasing unemployment & rising costs, having a steady income has become a critical issue nowadays. This has a direct bearing not only on the security and well-being of their children but also on the security of their retirement days. If you work at home on internet, not only will you be able to earn a steady income but also be with your kids in their growing years. Moreover, the more you earn now, the more secure their future will be. In such circumstances, if you plan to start a home-based internet business, it makes perfect sense.

But the problem lies in how to select the right internet home based business opportunity. The different ideas of top home internet business often confuse the mind and stop us from taking a quick and concrete decision regarding the best home businesses. Then there are questions regarding the viability of these top home internet business opportunity. Then, you are also doubtful whether the income generated from the work at home on internet opportunity be able to replace that from a fulltime job?

In addition to the reliability factor there is another question regarding the amount of investment. What would be the costs of starting work at home on internet business initiative? When the monetary return from top home internet businesses is uncertain, then there is no logic in starting one. Hence, selecting the right internet home based business is of critical importance.

One such work at home on internet business opportunity is internet affiliate marketing. There are innumerable companies offering reliable affiliate programs. And in most cases, the affiliate fees are either free or a basic minimum. The benefits of these home-based internet businesses are many. There are tensions regarding inventory buildup, or issues such as commercial property, licenses, and other related chores. You will be able to keep your total focus on how to market the product or business concept on your website.

After selecting the right affiliate program to start your internet-based home business, you should go about building your own website which will mark foray into home based small business.

Do not leave your internet home based business midway and change to stable but permanent job. This is the mistake most people in the work at home on internet do. Also don't expect that you will become successful in your top internet home internet business in a short span of time. So, stay put and works hard at your internet home business.

There are various benefits associated with internet-based home business. They also require a smaller investment than offline ones. But it requires equal dedication, ethics, and hard work to make it successful in this competitive world.

Blend your strengths into small business needs

If you are looking to start a small business of your own, there is a proven process that is necessary to start off with. Many creative people have great business ideas, but their approach to planning is ineffective and eventually flops. First and foremost, you must find a market that is a good size. Now what does this mean exactly? Finding a niche market that is a reasonable size entails pinpointing one that is big enough to make a profit but small enough for the resources of a small business and one that does not compete with large corporations.

Two main mistakes that entrepreneurs make in finding small markets are targeting a market that is too broad and targeting a niche that is already heavily exploited. What you decide to sell must connect product to target audience or you will not be successful.

To start off with, choose your own unique area of expertise. What are you good at? What do you have experience in? Use your education, your skills, and the people you know who could help you transform your idea into reality. If you have many areas of interest and are not sure which one would be the most profitable, a little more research will be needed. Consider how it will be possible to convert your education and skills into money-making opportunities. Research your surrounding marketplace to see what is needed in your area.

Now if you are trying to find small markets online, be forewarned that this can be tedious and time-consuming. You will first have to think of a list of possible target audiences, then take your first idea and research an exhaustive list of keywords and keyword phrases that people in that target audience are using for information on their desired product. Next, one must research all keywords and phrases for relevancy and then study which keywords on your list might lead to other niches that will need future researching.

Then, you need to compare all your keywords to web pages to evaluate the present competition. You will use all your information to narrow down your list to keywords and phrases that have the most online traffic and those that are the least exploited. If your small market does not appear to be profitable, you must start the entire research process over. If you do find one that seems to be a money maker, you then must focus on finding ideas to profit from.

Chapter 2 Success
Number one reason for failure

Nearly half of all small businesses fail within the first two years of operation. The number one reason for business failure is inadequate planning. The second reason is under-capitalization.

So, before you mortgage your house, or go into debt financing your business, you need to know if your business is going to do more than survive -- you want to know if it's good enough to thrive! Here are three things successful businesses that have stayed in business for five years or longer have in common:

1. **The idea**

   A successful business start-up always starts with an idea. Something that makes your business stand out from all the rest. So how do you know if you've got a good idea?

You've probably got a good idea if you can answer yes to any of the following questions: Does your idea provide the solution to a significant problem for your target market? Does it satisfy a need or want? Does it create an opportunity?

The most successful businesses either fix problems (either real or perceived), or they increase your customer's pleasure. They create a repeat need for a product or service among the target market.

2. **The market**

    Your chances of survival are better if you can answer the following questions with a yes: Is there already a market for your product or service? (It's much easier to fill a need than trying to create an entirely new market.) Can your target market afford to buy your products or services? (If they can't afford it, it doesn't matter how great it is, you won't sell any!) Will your target market perceive your product or service as valuable? (If they want it, but don't think it's worth what you're selling it for, you won't make any sales.)

3. **Your ability**

    Do you have the people, the resources, and the knowledge to be able to consistently provide your products or services to your target market? Can you maintain a competitive advantage? Do you have enough manpower? Can you purchase the supplies and materials you need over the long run?

Your first step always is to create a solid business plan. Your business plan is more than an essay on "Why I deserve to get funding for my idea" however. Don't spend all the time creating a business plan and then toss it in the bottom drawer of your desk. Your business plan should be a living, breathing roadmap that helps you make sure you're on course and reaching the goals that you set for your business.

The second step to business survival is getting enough financing. Although the term "bootstrap entrepreneur" describes most small business owners, having enough capital to be able to keep your business afloat is vital to your survival.

If finding financing is a problem, either because you don't have enough credit or equity, or there are other problems, take the time to investigate the resources that are available in your community. There are a wide variety of grants and loans (including microloans) for entrepreneurs, if you know where to look, such as Chamber of Commerce.

Find a mentor. Most entrepreneurs have great skills and abilities, but no one does everything well. You probably already know what your strengths and weaknesses are. (If not, there are many resources and tools that can help you figure it out!) Rather than ignoring your weaknesses, find a mentor who can help you either build your skills in your weaker areas, or offer advice for getting what you need.

Common mistakes in small business

When first starting your small business, you may not realize that there are mistakes you may make at different stages of your business' growth that can slowly kill it for months or even years if you don't watch out for them?

These mistakes are not just restricted to the new business owners. Many operating businesses, including those you may think are "successful" because they've been around for 10 years, are often still making them and are most likely losing a lot of money and/or wasting a lot of time in the process.

Although some of these mistakes seem aimed more at service type companies, they really do fit the bill for almost any type of business. Let's go over a few examples that you can use for future reference. Underestimating project or service time is a big one.

This relates to service companies as well as companies that sell a product. This is a service company's bread and butter. If you don't estimate the time and effort required to perform each service, your business offers you will lose out and there is little you can do about it except learn from it. The best way to estimate time required to do the job is to do it once yourself or watch your best employee perform the task, then determine the appropriate fees that you should charge for the service.

Not knowing your company numbers and setting prices to low. Notice I emphasized the word "your". It is a common mistake to use a competitor's fees as your pricing gauge without knowing why they use those numbers. Consider for a minute what will happen if you take a competitor's price, cut it by 10% and then start selling.

What if the competition has a bad pricing structure and is barely making money or even losing money? What if your costs are more than theirs? While it's a good idea to know your competitors pricing structure and maybe even use it as a starting point you shouldn't base your whole strategy on it.

Different market sectors have their own variables as far as costs go and you should be aware of them for your project or product pricing. What you pay for a product you are going to sell is not the only cost to have in your head when you are pricing your products. Considering how much your labor and materials cost for a service is only a part of an hourly rate.

Employees also cost more than just salary and not every employee is part of your labor cost. Every company has insurance to pay for. There are overhead expenditures, quality factors that need to be part of your pricing structure. What you include as "standard services" or "standard product features" as well as job site etiquette or in store service or warranties all need to go into your pricing.

Not charging for all your time and costs is mistake most business owners will admit that they made. For instance, let's say that you run a service company. You can't just undercut your competitor's price to acquire the job; you have to ensure that your costs will be covered in your rates. Stores undermine themselves, for example, when they put more people on the floor for customer service but don't charge for it. These things cost you money and when your competitors don't do them it costs them less money.

As a business owner you need to believe that you are providing your clients worthwhile wares that deserve to be paid for. If you get the chance to explain why your prices are higher, then take that opportunity and do it. If they don't like the fact that you include things that others charge extra for later or that you treat them better, then they are most likely completely price shoppers. You don't want them as regular customers anyway. Trust me.

Not getting paid fast enough is another one that easily creates a cash flow problem. If you are making enough money to pay the bills, this problem can be solved, prevented, or at least managed. To avoid this bill customers very promptly. After all that's the reason you are doing the work- to get paid.

Failure to have solid systems and procedures in place. Having no procedures and systems in place for tasks like billing, collections, payroll, interviewing, hiring, job responsibilities, manufacturing, operating equipment, maintaining equipment and inventory procedures will help things run smoothly and reduce expenditures as well.

Spending too much advertising money without tracking the results. There is no point in a marketing campaign if you do not put things in place that allow you to measure how well the plan is working.

Spreading yourself too thin is a classic mistake made by every entrepreneur. The key is to figure out when you are at that "wearing too many hats" point and start getting some help. Not getting help or waiting too long can kill a company. The three big issues people like to tackle themselves but are usually the ones they are the least knowledgeable about like: legal issues, accounting, bookkeeping and daily operations issues.

Keeping an eye out for these potential problems is always a good idea, the end of a year is an excellent time to make sure you are not making these errors. Take the time or make the time to determine if have issues to address. If you don't know how to stop or fix the mistakes, then find some help. The success of your business may depend on it!

Chapter 3 Protect your assets
Small business insurance

There are a lot of things that go into starting up and running a small business. One of the things that often gets set as a low priority is small business insurance. This, simply put, is a mistake. You are putting you and your business at risk every moment that you don't have insurance. It may take a bit of time and money to get insured, but it will cost a whole lot more if something should happen and you don't have insurance. In other words, you need to make it a priority.

The sad truth is that there are people out there who think all business owners have deep pockets...and that they should be sued for any reason or no real reason at all. Let's say someone has their shoelaces untied and trips on the sidewalk in front of your store. They could not only sue you, but if they have the right lawyer, they could win a lot of money. The worst part is that it doesn't matter if it's your fault or not. All that matters is how well a lawyer can convince a jury that you should pay for it.

Will they always win such cases? No, they won't. However, there is nothing stopping them from suing you and trying to win. That alone can get expensive, unless you have liability small business insurance. Just having to use it once will make the premium more than worth it.

As a small business owner, you don't only have to be concerned about liability, but also about theft. Stuff has a funny way of walking out the door when you own a business. You may be most worried about there being a major break-in after your business closes for the day. And while professional thieves may be a threat, the real problem is shoplifting and employee theft. They may not take as much at any one time, but those small thefts can really add up. Because it is a real threat, your small business insurance policy should cover theft.

You should also have a policy that covers you against fire and natural disasters. These are all things that could wipe out your business in minutes, and they often occur with very little or no warning. There's no question that it would be devastating to lose everything, but it would be even worse if you had no way of replacing it.

With how many things can potentially go wrong, small business insurance is a must. You should have a policy in place before you even open the doors, and you should consider it as a normal part of operating your business. If you already own a small business and don't have insurance, then get it as soon as you possibly can. It could end up saving you from all kinds of disasters; both man-made and natural.

Benefits of insurance

As a small business owner, insurance is probably one of the last things on your priority list. However, this is a big mistake and can end up costing you your business in the worst-case scenario or eating up your profits in the best case scenario. There are many benefits to taking out small business insurance and you will find that the costs offset themselves quite quickly.

1. Liability

Probably the most important benefit in taking out small business insurance is that you are covered for liability. Businesses make easy targets in case of onsite accidents. If someone is injured at your place of business and you don't have any form of liability insurance, you will end up paying for the rest of your life to cover medical expenses and any other damages the courts see fit to grant the person who was injured.

You may think that since you run a small office that there are no accidents your business can be found at fault for. However, even if someone just trips over a wire and twists an ankle in your office, they can sue you for damages and medical expenses. It really doesn't matter if it was their fault. The accident took place in your office so you are liable and since you are a business you will probably end up paying more than you could have imagined for a sprained ankle.

Small business insurance will cover you in all these situations, whether the person is a visitor, client, or employee.

2. Theft

Small business insurance will also cover you for the cost of equipment or goods that have been stolen. So, if you have a warehouse and goods are stolen because of a break-in your insurance policy will cover the cost of replacing the stolen property. This holds true for office equipment and any other property that you have insured.

The compensation you receive can save your business because having most of your inventory stolen can cause a serious dent in your turnover and profitability if you don't have coverage. Small business insurance will cover the costs and you can quickly replace your lost inventory.

3. Natural disasters

By taking out small business insurance against natural disasters you will be protecting your assets and inventory in case they are destroyed by natural disasters, such as a flood or earthquake.

If your place of business is destroyed by an earthquake, the costs of replacing everything can be staggering. A good insurance policy will cover the replacement costs so you can be up and running again in no time at all.

However, if you didn't have any small business insurance you will have to cover everything out of your own pocket. As most small business owners don't have massive financial backing and usually don't have such a large emergency reserve of funds it usually means that they end up filing for bankruptcy.

Taking out small business insurance can mean the difference between having a successful business and losing it all in a moment.

Property insurance

If you have a small business then to protect it from any loss due to mishaps, you need property insurance. Choosing property insurance for your small business is advised by all because it is key aspect in small business. To keep the small business together, property insurance plays a vital role. Property insurance ensures that your small business never falls apart.

There many risks involved with the small business, which cannot be eradicated or controlled. The source of revenue through the small business is threatened without a proper protection of property insurance. It provides the much-needed protection to eliminate perils involved with the small business.

Home property insurance is differed from the property insurance offered for small business.

To ensure the proper protection of your small business, you need to customize the property insurance package. Small business is a unique and these makes it vulnerable to the perils associated with it. You must design the property insurance according to desire, to achieve the complete protection of your small business.

There are three general areas, which are usually covered by almost all policies of property insurance: business interruption, professional liability, and property/contents.

Business Interruption Coverage

This is one of the important aspects of property insurance offered for small business. There are numerous factors that can interrupt the small business, like damage or any loss of property due to any mishaps. In such cases, property insurance compensates for the income, which is lost due to such causes. The policy of property insurance covers these losses or damage of property.

Professional Liability Coverage

Small business cannot run effectively without the policy of property insurance that covers the professional liability. The purpose of these policies of property insurance is to protect against the harm or injury to others, caused due to the negligence. For instance, customer or employee gets hurt due to the negligence in working hour or a consumer is injured. If the person chooses to sue you in lawsuit, then, property insurance coverage to this area will compensate for the lawsuit charges and fees. Also, the property insurance will pay for the fees of lawyer.

Product liability is a major feature that is directly related with the property insurance of small business. Property insurance of small business protects the policyholder from the losses or damages caused by the products, which could be injury caused by the product used by a consumer. If you are doctor, realtor, computer consultant or an architect, then property insurance for your small business would be suitable. The policy of property insurance will protect you from the error occurred from your side.

Property/Content Coverage

The policy of property insurance covers all the assets of your small business and provides protection for the property and the content. For instance, the property insurance offers protection from loss or damage of the building structure, and other contents related to any small business such as, equipment and facilities. Moreover, the policy of property insurance also offers protection against perils such as, theft, fire, or flood.

How to incorporate your business

If your small business is growing rapidly, you might consider incorporating the business to help it reach its full potential. To incorporate business is not difficult, but there is a process to follow. This step-by-step guide will help you get on the right track.

Prepare for Incorporation

To prepare for incorporation, first choose your primary business location. If your business operates in only one state, you will need to incorporate in that state. If your business operates in multiple states, then you have the option to choose which state to incorporate in, usually the state that's more business friendly when it comes to taxes and laws pertaining to business.

Next, select a name for your corporation. Check with your Secretary of State to make sure the name you choose is not already taken by another company. Also, do research online to be sure the name is not taken by another business and doesn't have a patent by another company or individual. Once you're sure the name is free to use, you can register your company name. The name will likely need to be registered as "Doing Business As" or "DBA."

Choose a Filing Agent

The next step is to decide who will register your corporation, receive forms for incorporation, and file your paperwork. The least expensive route is to do all paperwork yourself, but if you're completely new to incorporation, you'll benefit tremendously by hiring an agent. The agent must live in the state where you will incorporate the business. The agent may be an attorney who provides incorporation services, or the agent can be a service that specializes in incorporation. Hiring a service is usually far less expensive than hiring an attorney.

Develop a Corporate Structure

Whether you're the only member or shareholder of your company or you already have multiple shareholders, you should determine a corporate structure before registering the corporation. To structure the company means to determine how the stock will be spread among shareholders along with other rights such as voting rights and finances. Be sure everyone agrees with the structure and put everything in writing before filing your paperwork to incorporate the company.

Next, put together your corporate by-laws, or a set of rules that determine how board members will be elected, their duties, how and when board meetings are to be held, and other important details of how the corporation will be operated.

Ready to File

Now you're ready to obtain an Employee Identification Number (EIN) and select a board of directors for your company. Once these two tasks are accomplished, check to be sure you have all necessary paperwork and check the company name availability once again to be on the safe side. Now, you're ready to file your corporate paperwork for registration.

Forming an LLC - Know the Difference

Keep in mind that forming a corporation differs from forming an LLC (Limited-Liability Company). When you form an LLC, your business will be treated as a sole proprietorship or partnership under federal and state tax laws. You will be required to report profits and losses, income, credits, and deductions on your individual tax return.

Corporations, on the other hand, pay taxes on the company's profits. The shareholders are treated as individual employees, and each receive their own salaries and file their personal tax returns separately. LLC formation requires less paperwork and has fewer legal issues than a corporation.

If you're pressed for time and want to get things moving quickly with your company's incorporation, there are websites available to help you incorporate online. These sites provide printable paperwork, state-by-state instructions, and other helpful items to make it easier than ever to incorporate your business.

Taxes and your small business

Every small business owner worry about paying taxes and looks for ways of reducing their tax burden. When you have a small business of your own you must keep up date on your knowledge of tax laws that pertain to "small businesses." You must also clearly understand accounting systems and tax planning.

The best place to start is to sit down with your accountant and plan the different ways that you will maintain business expenses, filing receipts, "tax saving" investments, and a strategy for running your business in the most beneficial way.

Did you know that?...

According to law you can reduce your tax liability by hiring family members to carry out work in your business. Pay your children and spouse to perform assigned duties. This way you can shift from higher tax rates to lower ones.

Hiring independent contractors instead of employees. You will save on payroll taxes. However, ensure that you meet the IRS's criteria.

You can take advantage of tax deductions allowed for charitable donations. Make donations in November or December instead of January so that you can include the donations for tax deductions in the current year.

You can maximize your expenditure on equipment and office supplies. Buy in advance for a quarter and use the tax deductions allowed in the current fiscal year.

If you pay all bills due before the end of the year. Payment to cell services, rent, insurance, and utilities related to the business can be included for accounting and applicable tax waivers.

By setting up a retirement plan and making payments before the end of the year. This will reduce your income for the year and proportionately the tax due. Be sure to check on the limits. Plan a feasible and beneficial strategy with your accountant.

Be sure to deduct from your taxable income money paid to licensing fees, businesses taxes, and annual memberships to businesses related organizations. Be sure to deduct interest paid on borrowings for running the business and related fees. Insurance premiums paid to ensure the business office and machinery are eligible for tax deductions. Make a list of your memberships and check which ones are eligible for tax deductions.

Check whether you have deducted management and administration expenses as well as money spent on maintenance and repairs of equipment.

Decide whether you should use a cash accounting system or accrual one. Which one will benefit your business the most? Keep in mind that the tax deductions are different depending on the system you use.

When setting up your small business it is wise to seek out the advice of a tax and accounting professional as to which accounting system would be most suitable.

Chapter 4 Financial
How to finance your small business

If you have a great business idea or plan, or you would like to expand your existing business, don't let a lack of funds stop you in your tracks. There is a wide variety of financing available for small businesses. Let's look at the financing opportunities that small business entrepreneurs can take advantage of.

While the financing sources comprise diverse institutions, such as banks, government sources, venture capitalist and "angel" investors, it is useful to look at what all lenders, regardless of category, want when they loan money or invest in a business enterprise.

When you seek money for an already existing business, lenders will be interested to know about the history of your business, whether it has a track record of good management and good performance. Your credit history will also be under scrutiny. A good credit history will help you to get a loan.

You can also bolster your chances of getting a loan by putting up collateral. This reduces the risk for the bank in case you default. And finally, if you can show that your own personal money is invested in your enterprise then lenders will have more confidence in the proposition.

Many small business loans are turned down due to poorly presented proposals, inadequate collateral, insufficient cash flow and a lack of management experience.

These are the general points that lenders and investors are interested in, now let's look at the main sources for small business financing.

1. Traditional Lenders: Banks, credit unions, and finance companies are the main source of loans to small businesses. Many of these institutions have a small-business department and are experienced in handling small-business loans. The most logical place to start is with the institution which handles your business and personal banking.

2. Government Sources, the Small Business Administration (SBA): The programs of the SBA work in conjunction with the traditional lenders, as they are mostly loan guarantee programs that reduce the risk to lenders in case of default. Some of the popular SBA programs are as follows

   a. The 7(a)-loan guarantee program: This program helps businesses which lack sufficient collateral, by providing repayment guarantees ranging from 75-85% depending on the size of the loan.

   b. The SBA Low Doc loan program: There is only one form to fill out for these loans and approval time is rapid (within 36 hours from when the SBA receives the applications. These loans are only for amounts up to $15,000 but they can be used for start-up businesses.

c. The SBA Express loan program: This is another quick-procedure loan guarantee program, but it covers loans up to $250,000. The SBA guarantees 50% of these loans, and interest rates in this program may be higher than in the other SBA programs

3. Venture Capitalists: These are typically firms that are seeking investment opportunities in companies with a high profit potential. Usually when you take money from a Venture Capitalist firm it means that you have to give up some ownership and control to the investors. If you are thinking of going in this direction, then it is imperative to investigate the VC firm, and make sure that it has good references.

4. Angel Investors: These are individual investors who are looking for good opportunities in a wide variety of businesses. You don't have to be a high-tech company to attract these funds. Angels have smaller sums to invest than venture capitalists, and their investments range from $100,000 to $1 Million.

Prepare your proposal carefully and approach the institutions or individuals that best match your needs and capacity.

Private investors

Private investors for startup small businesses may not be a dime in a dozen these days, but if you've truly a worthwhile idea for business to propose then there's nothing to worry about. Speak the right words at the right time and place to the right person and you can get yourself some takers!

How to Find Potential Private Investors for Small Businesses

When looking for potential investors, it's important to remember how critical each opportunity is that comes your way. Also, don't underestimate but don't take unreasonable risks either. If you know you've got a genuine money-making opportunity in your hands, there's no need to be desperate.

Personal Network

Your personal network is made up of family, friends, and close colleagues. All these may be able to refer a name or two so take the time to explain your situation and ask for their help. This isn't the time for stubborn pride or inhibitions.

News

Scour the business news for mentions of well-known entrepreneurs, venture capitalists, angel investors, and the likes. The type of business you'd propose may not be in league with the kind of projects they commonly involve their selves in, but there's no harm in trying, is there?

Advertise

If there's no way for you to reach potential private investors, then try doing it the other way around. Make them come to you instead by advertising. Of course, you'll need to pick the right vehicles for approaching them. Mere classifieds won't be enough. Give a hint or two to your bank manager, offer compensation in exchange for a little help, and there's sure to be a little bird able to whisper to the right ears about your business proposal.

What to Say to Potential Private Investors for Startup Small Businesses

Getting an appointment with a potential private investor is just the beginning. The next step is harder…and more important. You need to convince them to risk their money by investing in your proposed business. To do that, you need to focus on the factors listed below.

Products or Services

To know thy product (service) is to know thy business. Ultimately, everything will come down to what you're selling. You need to know every feature of your product or service, how it fares against the competition, what its main attraction is to your market, and what could enable your products or services to triumph.

Give them proof. Let them know why you're convinced people will buy them and you're sure to win them over!

Target Market

Of course, having excellent products or services to sell won't be enough to make your business survive, much less profit. You're sure to impress potential private investors more if you come prepared with a list of well-thought-of strategies and tactics for marketing your products and services. They want to see how well you comprehend your target market and how effective and efficient you are at applying your knowledge to generate profit for your business.

ROI (Return On Investment)

Think rate and term. Firstly, they want to know exactly how long it would take them to recoup their investment. Secondly, they want to know how much more they can earn from their investment. Approximate figures won't do. You need to calculate the odds, provide projected figures, and tell them simply if they can become richer – or poorer – because of your startup business.

Unsecured start up loans

First-time small business owners usually are chary of unsecured start up loans. This is because the time frame for making a profit is not definite whether there is a properly thought out and lucrative business plan in place for the future business.

When profits or revenues do not materialize per plans, as in most cases, there is danger of default on loan repayment. When this happens credit rating of the person involved gets degraded as unsecured loans are granted based on credit and borrowing history of the business owner.

And if there is bad credit history behind, he/she can very well forget that small business loan. Let's discuss some more aspects of unsecured small business startup loans.

Some Facts

If the credit history of 'to be' small business owner is good, unsecured start-up business loans are easier to avail as compared to other business loans. But it is better to go for secured loans against property or equipment affiliated with the business.

Secured loan not only keeps personal credit rating intact but poses lesser risks for the business owners, because they can use the hypothecated equipment to generate a profit for the business. As a result, the loan can be paid back on time. Not just that, secured loans are for longer tenure and come with lesser interest rate burden, thereby lowering the cost of loan.

But if you have decided to apply for unsecured small business start-up loans, you should be careful about the requested amount. Remember, the more you owe on the loan (including interest), the more will be the money which you have to repay.

If you are not exactly sure how well the business will do in the first year and want to keep your credit rating good, it is best to request a small amount for your unsecured start-up business loan. This will make sure that repayment installments are small and if you are punctual in repaying, you can always ask for more, which will be gladly given.

Before you apply for an unsecured business start-up loan, there are several things that you should keep in mind.

First, you will need to convince the lender that it is a good decision to issue the loan to you. Since unsecured loans are based on your credit and repayment history, you will have to convince lenders that you can handle your personal finances in an organized fashion. Good credit record will put lenders at ease since they will be able to see your repayment history on your credit report.

Since lenders will be looking at your credit report, you should maintain a positive report as far as possible. If you know that you owe certain lenders, you should try to settle these debts or set up a payment plan with your creditors. This will be visible on your report.

Before you make any final decisions about unsecured start-up loans for business, be sure to speak to an accountant or a representative from your local bank. This will make sure that you are applying for the right loans which would help your business to develop quickly and steadily. You must not take a decision unless you are convinced.

Various financing options

There are numerous challenges when establishing your own small business. Financing is a major aspect to consider when embarking on this journey. Determining where the funds are going to come from can sometimes turn out to be a very nerve-racking endeavor.

This really is an obvious obstacle, that you must overcome, and one, which often prevents many people from starting their own small business.

Bank loans are usually the first step that most people take when attempting to start their own small business. Banking institutions can become demanding for things like collateral and business plans. Banks do tend to make it hard for the people attempting to start their own business. The demand for personal assets and the thought of putting your home up for collateral can be stressful and scary at the same time.

Banks can also demand that the business owner rent their business space as compared to purchasing the space. They make these demands occasionally because they do not want you to tie up their money in assets that in the bank's eyes will offer no short-term rewards. Banks may even demand that you use their money for inventory, which will offer them some immediate returns in case of closure. You must also keep in mind that these loans come with interest charges that will increase the amount that you must repay.

Applying for government grants is something I recommend to every person interested in starting their own small business. The US as well as other countries has numerous programs that cater to the needs of potential small business owners. Make sure you check not only the federal government but also your local state and state government as well for possible grants, which could aid you in your venture. Applying for a grant is not an easy task, but it is well worth the effort because the money does not have to be repaid.

When it comes to relatives or friends you may be reluctant to ask to borrow money to start your small business, but this is sometimes a good option because they are obviously people who know and trust you. The only downside to this suggestion of relatives or friends is that they may feel that they own a stake in your business, so it is important that you keep the terms clear from the beginning.

This type of loan often has no legal binding; however, it can create serious rifts between you and your loved ones. Be sure you point out that the money is only a loan and will by no means give them any share or say in your new small business.

Dipping into your own personal funds is another way to fund your small business. This is typically used with a combination of other methods. The great thing about this approach is that you will not be confronted with interest charges and personal conflicts that other loans may demand.

One more option to consider is accepting private donations or seeking out investors. If you feel you have a great new idea for a new small business, it is possible to sell your great idea to potential investors; these are commonly called venture capitalists.

Unlike receiving loans from your family members, this method will without a doubt involve the investor having some type of stake in your business. The disadvantage of this method is that the idea must be creative as well as potentially profitable because you literally have to convince the investors that you are going to make money.

Often a controlling interest in the company will be given if an investor spends their money for you to start your own small business, so you must be prepared to share control of your business to some extent.

Whichever way you decide to fund your small business it is important that you do your research and be ready to face any obstacles that may get in your way.

The importance of a business credit card

Small business plays a vital role in today's economy. It is now easier than ever to establish a new business. According to the US Small Business Administration, small businesses pay over 45% of the US private payroll. Small businesses also employ over half of all private sector employees and provide 60-80 percent of new jobs. With millions of small businesses in the US alone, virtually all financial institutions now offer small business loans to qualifiers for a percentage. So why apply for a small business credit card?

Keep Track of All Your Small Business Expenses
The first and most obvious reason for a small business credit card is to separate personal finances from business related purchases. With your small business credit card, you can make all your transactions by phone, internet or in person. Then get periodic statements detailing all your business expenses.

Business credit cards are accepted virtually everywhere that you shop. Covering business purchases with employee's personal money can get very messy. So instead of relying on cash, use a business credit card. Most credit card issuers offer a credit limit for employee cards as well as different methods to monitor how the card is used.

You no longer must dread the year-end nightmare of trying to track where and when you spent your money. It's like having all your book-keeping done automatically for you! In a digital world, why should your business have to collect every printed receipt?

Establish Your Small Business
A credit card with your business name on it gives your business credibility. A business credit card looks a lot more professional than paying from your own wallet. It also gains the respect of financial institutions. Just by owning a business credit card, your business can build credit. So, when you need that business loan, you will get the best interest rate and qualify for higher amounts. As your credit builds you might also qualify for a lower interest business credit card.

So even if your business doesn't have a 6-figure budget, a business credit card could help your business grow. You never know when your business might suddenly need extra money. Office equipment might need immediate replacement. Without a business credit card, financing could drastically interfere with your daily routine.

Earn Rewards with a Business Credit Card

You can also save money and earn rewards. Certain business credit cards give you cash back on all your purchases. Other cards give you varying cash back percentages depending on where you shop…gas stations, grocery stores, office supply stores, etc. A cash back business credit card is a great way to increase your profit margin.

Other cards give you airline travel rewards just for using your credit card. For instance, if your company has frequent business plane trips, then small business credit cards that offer travel miles, hotel accommodations or travel insurance are most suitable. This type of credit card could give you travel discounts, free flights, free companion travel or upgraded flight seating.

Not only does a small business credit card provide convenience and rewards, but it also helps to build business credit for the future of your company as you watch it grow! Research the business credit cards available and find the card that best suits your business needs. Finance your business for today and tomorrow.

Commercial credit counseling

Do you own a small business? In these difficult economic times, you may be suffering from additional cash flow pressures. Have you considered commercial credit counseling?

A lot of small business owners face similar predicaments. They are fantastic at promoting their services and are often experts in their field but very few of them know enough about finance to run a business properly. All business owners should be able to produce a profit and loss account, a cash flow statement, and a balance sheet. I am not suggesting that you become an accountant or a bookkeeper but unless you fully understand these basic accountancy principles you run the risk of letting your business fail.

Yes, you can employ people to do these tasks for you and this is a great idea as I am a firm believer in playing to your strengths. BUT you still need to understand and know how to read a set of accounts. Otherwise, you could find yourself the victim of fraud. As the business owner, you are ultimately responsible for filing the correct forms and tax returns. The IRS will not accept any excuses including the fact that you let your accountant handle things. So, protect yourself by educating yourself in the basics of business finance.

When you deal with a commercial credit counseling service, their staff are experts at teaching business owners how best to manage their business finances. They will advise on the best place to hold cash investments, how much to hold on instant access banking facilities and how much they could afford to tie up for a while. They will also help find the best deals on any form of credit your business may need be it a business loan, short term cash flow injection or factoring of your debtor's book.

They will review your company accounts and give you advice on how you are handling your debtors and creditors. Often small business owners will extend credit for too long and this can have an adverse effect on your cash flow. Also, the longer the debts are outstanding the more risk there is of them not being repaid in full. Your counselor will be able to advise you on how best to offer credit terms without risking losing your customers or your income.

Your business finances should always be kept separate from your personal finances even if the business itself is a sole trader as opposed to a separate legal entity. Steer clear of any commercial credit counseling service who tries to manage your personal affairs as well. You want their expertise on the business side, but it would be better to have someone who is an expert on personal finance manage your own money.

Check the prices and quality of services on offer at your local firm. Ask your business contacts for recommendations i.e., who do they use for their commercial credit counseling services and why. Recommendations are often the best way of finding experts who can help you make the most of your business.

Chapter 5 ECommerce

E commerce development

Owning a small business currently is becoming more difficult. The fact is that major franchises, chains, and large stores are taking over the little guys out there. Every day in every small town, people witness the little shops, stores and service providers slipping into the cracks and closing shop. This is sad, especially with all the tools and resources available on the internet. Using the internet is just another method of advertising, a newer tool in the toolbox that these small businesses can use to increase their annual revenue and remain open for business.

Not that the internet is a new tool, it's simply not, but it is new to a lot of small business owners out in the country struggling to stay alive. To many small business owners, computers and the internet are a scary and uncharted territory for them. These business owners have a false sense of cost and productivity that having a web presence can bring. Not only is it essential to have a website in today's changing market, but it is also essential to have an ecommerce website that sells all of the products and services a business offers. Trends are leaning towards people using the internet as their own personal tool at home to look for the perfect car, house, mop, jewelry, anything really. Sitting at home and browsing is a lot less intrusive than going out in a car to the store, especially with the costs of gas going up, to find exactly what they are looking for.

Why not use this semi-new tool, the internet, to grow your business online and reach a much larger target audience for your products and services? Having an online presence is not enough of a tool, if you provide either a service or good (merchandise) and it can be used worldwide, then you need to present that to the world. You may just find as a small business owner, that providing vital information, services and goods to the larger online public is a very lucrative and smart business decision.

How would a small business go about getting an ecommerce developed website? Search that powerful tool again, the internet. Find a reputable web design firm that specializes in ecommerce development and ecommerce shopping cart solutions. Pick a web design firm that provides high quality work but thinks about designing an ecommerce website driven from just the "design" point of view. Your ecommerce website does need to look professional, but more importantly it needs to flow and function properly. Your visitors should be able to decide from your navigation what area of your website that interests them the most. Your visitors should be able to use your online tools, navigation, and shopping cart easily without confusion or error.

It is more than important to develop a properly working ecommerce website. If you are not utilizing this great tool, the internet, to your small businesses advantage, then you are most certainly missing out on sales, leads and customers. Owning a small business doesn't mean you have to fade away when the next big chain store settles in next door to you. Fight back, with the fairest tool around, the internet. Get your small business a website that has the ecommerce power to reach all your target demographic audience and watch your money roll on in.

E commerce web sites

In first World countries the Internet is now a huge part of our everyday life. We use it at work, and we use it at home. It is all around us. A person from a First World country would be in a minority if they said they had not paid for anything across the Internet or bought a product or service online through an eCommerce store.

One study found that residents in European Nations spent $132 Billion Euros (USD $180 Billion) through eCommerce Websites. In the next 5 years the amount spent through eCommerce Websites is set to increase by 25% per annum to an estimated $406.8 Billion Euros (USD $554 Billion). It should be noted this only covers Europe and does not factor in the US, Asia, and other emerging regions, which would easily double or triple those figures.

So, clearly there is a huge marketplace online that needs to be serviced by online shops and websites selling products and services. As a business owner I can see a huge market for established businesses in the real World to move into the World of eCommerce and sell online.

ECommerce Website Partners should be assessed for their suitability to deliver a quality ongoing relationship that will be to your company's best benefit for the long term.

1. A strong history of developing eCommerce Websites with a good portfolio and testimonials

2. Hosting with reliable and strong Internet connections

3. Good design and development team adequate support in the future

4. Online Marketing Professionals with proven history of success and a good portfolio of established clients - THE single most important feature of any shop - getting visitors through the doors!

As a business owner I would describe an eCommerce store with Search Engine Optimization implemented as a store with many, many different doorways into it. ECommerce websites owners should recognize that the more people you get to come to your website the more sales you will make. Search Engine Optimization does exactly this, targeting certain phrase that when searched on in Google your website shows up for. Now it should be noted that the higher to the top you finish the more website visitors you are likely to get.

It has been shown in studies that 80% of all people who search on a term go to one, or more, of the results on the first page (the top 10) results. So, the goal with SEO is to get on the first page and in the top 10 results shown for a given search term. So your goal in choosing a partner should be focused on good website design but more on online marketing and how they can help you spread the word and get visitors to your website.

An eCommerce website provides many benefits to the underlying business. It gives the business an extra dimension and as mentioned above if implemented with SEO, many doorways into the shop. With more customers comes more revenues - everyone recognizes this fact. An eCommerce Shop also provides Interstate, National and even global reach for your product or service. With a Global eCommerce system, you can reach the farthest reaches of the World and supply product, creating a Global Brand Name in new emerging markets.

Do small businesses need web site?

When the experts tell you you're going to need a press kit for your small business I'll bet you're wondering why on earth you'd need one. At least, I think you'd wonder why if you think a press kit is just for the press. But the term 'press kit' is misleading if you ask me because press kits aren't just what their name implies.

I prefer to call them small business information kits or information packages instead because that's what they really are. They are meant to inform everyone, not just the press about you and your business.

Once you have a small business information kit, you'll find you're often giving them when someone asks for information about your company--who you are, what you do, how you can benefit them. In fact, you'll probably find you'll give out almost as many of your information kits as your business cards.

Sometimes it's more appropriate to simply hand out just your card, but other times, you might like to give someone more information than what's on your business card.

Say you're at a party and someone asks what you do. You'd probably just give them your business card. But your business card gives this business contact only the briefest information about your company.

So, you might also ask for their name and address, and send them an information kit the next day. Sending your information kit, the next day also works as an important reminder of the evening's discussion.

On the other hand, if you're a plumbing company, you might want to contact construction companies in your area to see if they're interested in subcontracting your company from time to time, or better yet all the time!

Sending them just a business card probably won't get you very far. Even sending a well-written letter introducing your company together with your business card probably wouldn't be as effective as a complete information kit.

You could think of your business card as the "who and the where, and a little bit of the what" of the 6 interview questions—who, what, where, when why and how. Your card probably has your business name, contact information and possibly a slogan, motto or some saying suggesting what you do.

Your information kit on the other hand, answers all the questions. It tells people who and where you are, just like your business card does. But instead of one little line suggesting what you do, your information kit tells people exactly what you do. How well it tells them what you do depends on how good your copywriting is.

The real secret is convincing people they can't do without your product or service, remembering that along with a great description of your product or service, to consider your information kit from your clients' perspective. Everyone wants to know how what you do can benefit them. How you can save them time or how you can save them money, or how you can make their life just a little bit easier.

One last word on presentation of your small business identity package. It's almost as important as what you say. A professional image can go a long way in assuring potential clients your small business is the one they want to do business with.

You cannot compete with big companies without one, and you'll be miles ahead of the small businesses that don't have one. And while we're talking about professional image, imagine how your small business will be perceived when you have the ultimate in professional image-- a matching corporate identity package, information kit and small business web site.

The value of web presence

Undoubtedly, the internet can make the difference between a successful small business, and one ignored by customers. Due to the global nature of the Internet surpassing physical frontiers between nations, and even making it unnecessary to use printed business cards when they can easily be hosted online.

Web presence can make small businesses more competitive from any angle, allowing you to understand new trends, as well as discover opportunities and problems without wasting time. A small business with Internet presence improves your opportunity to connect with several suppliers and customers that otherwise might not be possible in your local area.

Furthermore, traditional printed business cards including an Internet address, not only opens a new range of possibilities to succeed, but also is a way to increase your communications, showing an appealing professional appearance, no matter how big or small your business or company is. Magnetic business cards often create a long-lasting marketing image.

In fact, you will be surprised to see prospective clients seeking what they want through search engines. Others might check for URLs in business cards instead of browsing the printed yellow pages, because a web presence translates is synonym to having a shop or booth in every corner of the world, where every individual or small business can have the same presence as the big enterprises.

Of course, budget, skills, knowledge, and other Internet resources determine the performance of every small business online. However, it will always be beneficial to develop your business web presence if you want to get customers from every location around the world or, as a practical alternative, you can create online business cards for you, your partners, and employees.

On the Internet, you will find several websites offering both services, development of your web presence and creating your online business cards, ranging from low-mid prices to those unaffordable for people who are just starting a new business venture. However, you do not need a big budget to start.

There are several free Web hosting services that will gladly give you web space to develop your presence. If you have no idea how to create a website, they usually have facilities called online tools or web site builders, allowing you to create a nice-looking page with just a small amount of information regarding your small business, products and services.

If you do not feel comfortable with those tools, there are other options for you. If you want to create only a business card that looks like real printed business cards, you can always get free or cheap web templates, coming in a variety of designs and only requiring your information to be uploaded, which will create your web presence instantly.

Chapter 6 Branding
How to effectively brand your business

Branding a small business is a must if you want to succeed in a competitive world. The importance of branding a business disregarding its size is based on not only real benefits, products, and services that your business possesses, but also an image concept that all businesses should keep in mind.

From color business cards to global business identity, depending on how effectively you brand your business, the more or the less opportunities of success will knock at your door. The reason why large companies brand their businesses is because they know this is the best way to differentiate their products and services from their competitors while creating a corporate image.

Many small business owners believe it is not necessary to development a corporate image, particularly those whose business integrate just a few individuals as staff, or even when they own a one-man business, using the internet for selling or promoting their professional services. However, even a small business should utilize the same principles as the large enterprises to brand their business.

Furthermore, if your business has business cards, stationery and other branded elements along with a matching website, you will not only create a corporate image, but also loyal relationships with your customers and prospective customers, who will find more reliability with a small business with these characteristics, than others without a professional look and feel.

Because you only can impress new customers once, you should make sure that this impression is a positive and lasting introduction and handshake, only possible if you brand your business conveniently and professionally. There is no need to spend thousands of dollars to achieve it, but do not go to the other extreme using uneven elements.

Small businesses should be aware of the elements that will make their brand unique and recognizable, including consistency between online and printed elements, such as your logo, signage, business cards and even a slogan that helps people understand briefly your business's mission statement.

Effective branding must achieve these goals; be consistent and never differing, carrying the same logo, colors, slogans, and statements through to every element of your business, all of them always visible and unique, hence the need to avoid elements that anyone can find anywhere such as free or cheap clipart.

Creating your brand, whatever your budget requires a business plan to have a solid appreciation on whom your customers will be and what can you do to serve them. This is not only a matter of elegant stationary or catchy business cards; it is the most important deployment of a small business for an eventual growth in future terms.

Does a small business need a press kit?

When the experts tell you you're going to need a press kit for your small business I'll bet you're wondering why on earth you'd need one. At least, I think you'd wonder why if you think a press kit is just for the press. But the term 'press kit' is misleading if you ask me because press kits aren't just what their name implies.

I prefer to call them small business information kits or information packages instead because that's what they really are. They are meant to inform everyone, not just the press about you and your business.

Once you have a small business information kit, you'll find you're often giving them when someone asks for information about your company--who you are, what you do, how you can benefit them. In fact, you'll probably find you'll give out almost as many of your information kits as your business cards.

Sometimes it's more appropriate to simply hand out just your card, but other times, you might like to give someone more information than what's on your business card.

Say you're at a party and someone asks what you do. You'd probably just give them your business card. But your business card gives this business contact only the briefest information about your company.

So, you might also ask for their name and address, and send them an information kit the next day. Sending your information kit, the next day also works as an important reminder of the evening's discussion.

On the other hand, if you're a plumbing company, you might want to contact construction companies in your area to see if they're interested in subcontracting your company from time to time, or better yet all the time!

Sending them just a business card probably won't get you very far. Even sending a well-written letter introducing your company together with your business card probably wouldn't be as effective as a complete information kit.

You could think of your business card as the "who and the where, and a little bit of the what" of the 6 interview questions — who, what, where, when why and how. Your card probably has your business name, contact information and possibly a slogan, motto or some saying suggesting what you do.

Your information kit on the other hand, answers all the questions. It tells people who and where you are, just like your business card does. But instead of one little line suggesting what you do, your information kit tells people exactly what you do. How well it tells them what you do depends on how good your copywriting is.

The real secret is convincing people they can't do without your product or service, remembering that along with a great description of your product or service, to consider your information kit from your clients' perspective. Everyone wants to know how what you do can benefit them. How you can save them time or how you can save them money, or how you can make their life just a little bit easier.

One last word on presentation of your small business identity package. It's almost as important as what you say. A professional image can go a long way in assuring potential clients your small business is the one they want to do business with.

You cannot compete with big companies without one, and you'll be miles ahead of the small businesses that don't have one. And while we're talking about professional image, imagine how your small business will be perceived when you have the ultimate in professional image-- a matching corporate identity package, information kit and small business web site.

Chapter 7 Marketing
Internet marketing for small business

So, what is Internet marketing for small business all about? It is about defining who your target market is and then creating a relationship with that target market.

Once you do this then the sky is the limit for you and your bottom line.

Start your Internet marketing for small business by taking some time to think about who it is that will buy your product or service. Then think long and hard about how you can get the word out that you are the best provider of that product or service.

To get people to your website you need to be visible online. To get visible online you need to be optimized to the search engines. This is the best way for those people who can benefit from your wares to find you.

Once they find you need to grab their attention and then strive to do all you can to keep their attention. This is where you might run into some difficulty if you are not set up right.

Make sure that you have an opt-in form on every single page of your website so when potential customers find you, they can fill in the blanks with their contact information.

Once you have their contact information you should be able to follow up with them on a regular basis, so they continue to remember who you are and that you have what they need.

Offer a free report of some kind relating to your niche or product or service when they sign up so they are getting something of value from you right off the bat.

Don't just expect them to come running to you when they get to the point of making a purchase. You must cultivate this relationship and the best way to do that is to have an autoresponder set up.

What an autoresponder does is keep in touch with your email list every week or so, whenever you choose to have the emails sent out so you can cultivate the relationships.

People will more often buy from someone they know. It is said that it takes seven separate "meetings" for someone to think they know someone else and to trust them and the things they have to offer. Especially when it comes to making purchases online.

An autoresponder will help you do that. Say you want to send out emails to your list every week. What you must do is sit down once a month and write out four separate emails. Include things like discount offers or coupons to entice your readers even further.

Then enter them into the autoresponder and they get sent out when you have chosen each one to go out to your list. Easy.

You will have to pay something every month for the service of having the autoresponder, but it will increase traffic to your business exponentially and you will hardly notice the cost at all.

This is only one aspect of Internet marketing for small business. There is more to learn and master but always strive to keep in touch with your email list so they can come to you when they need you.

Small business internet marketing techniques

Small business internet marketing isn't just advertising anymore. It used to consist of purchasing ads in various places, and then purchasing specific types of ads, when the internet exploded. Now the difference between advertising and marketing has become very clear. Advertising is something you do that's very passive. Yes, you'll use specific language in any advertising space you purchase to try to entice people to click and buy, but once you've put the ad in place, it's there and it's not going to change. Even pay-per-click advertising falls into this more passive category.

But with many of the techniques of small business internet marketing, the things you do are far from passive. If you search engine optimize your website, that might seem passive because once you do it, it's done. But that's not true. As you add new pages to your website, you do more tweaking and changing. You'll use new keywords and different keywords in different areas. Sure, if you use banner ads you'll change them from time to time, but it's still much more static that almost any other type of marketing you can do.

And unless you have a huge advertising budget, those static ads like banners and pay-per-clicks probably aren't going to garner you many sales. It's the dynamic methods of small business internet marketing that are going to bring people to your website and keep them coming back. And when they keep coming back, they're once again faced with the things you offer. It can take a person 6 or 7 times seeing an offer before they're inclined to buy, so the more you get them at your website, seeing your products and services, the more likely it is you'll make a paying customer out of them.

The most efficient, active method of small business internet marketing that's guaranteed to let you make frequent contact with your target market is an opt-in mailing list. You can offer some information, a discount, or an ongoing thing like a 5-day course in something relevant to your site to get people to sign up for the mailing list. Once they've done that, you have their permission to send emails that will contain links and sales language designed to get them to go to your website and buy.

You won't want to just start sending ads every day. Come up with something that the people who found your website were probably looking for. If your small business internet marketing plan makes it likely that people will come across your website when looking for ways to keep aphids off houseplants, for instance, then offer a 3- 5- or 7- day email "course" about how take care of African violets or how to keep houseplants healthy in less-than-ideal conditions.

Small business internet marketing advice

Small business internet marketing isn't just advertising anymore. It used to consist of purchasing ads in various places, and then purchasing specific types of ads, when the internet exploded. Now the difference between advertising and marketing has become very clear. Advertising is something you do that's very passive. Yes, you'll use specific language in any advertising space you purchase to try to entice people to click and buy, but once you've put the ad in place, it's there and it's not going to change. Even pay-per-click advertising falls into this more passive category.

But with many of the techniques of small business internet marketing, the things you do are far from passive. If you search engine optimize your website, that might seem passive because once you do it, it's done. But that's not true. As you add new pages to your website, you do more tweaking and changing. You'll use new keywords and different keywords in different areas. Sure, if you use banner ads you'll change them from time to time, but it's still much more static that almost any other type of marketing you can do.

And unless you have a huge advertising budget, those static ads like banners and pay-per-clicks probably aren't going to garner you many sales. It's the dynamic methods of small business internet marketing that are going to bring people to your website and keep them coming back. And when they keep coming back, they're once again faced with the things you offer. It can take a person 6 or 7 times seeing an offer before they're inclined to buy, so the more you get them at your website, seeing your products and services, the more likely it is you'll make a paying customer out of them.

The most efficient, active method of small business internet marketing that's guaranteed to let you make frequent contact with your target market is an opt-in mailing list. You can offer some information, a discount, or an ongoing things like a 5-day course in something relevant to your site to get people to sign up for the mailing list. Once they've done that, you have their permission to send emails that will contain links and sales language designed to get them to go to your website and buy.

You won't want to just start sending ads every day. Come up with something that the people who found your website were probably looking for. If your small business internet marketing plan makes it likely that people will come across your website when looking for ways to keep aphids off of houseplants, for instance, then offer a 3- 5- or 7- day email "course" about how take care of African violets or how to keep houseplants healthy in less-than-ideal conditions.

Give them something of value, and they'll give you permission to contact them. Once you have that permission, good small business internet marketing will include emails that contain not just ads, but content to remind them what a valuable resource your website is.

Low-cost advertising

Advertising is key to a company's success, particularly in the beginning, when it has not garnered enough support from customers. There are many ways of advertising that are low cost. According to nfib.com, you can "Set up online accounts on local business directories, such as Yelp and Yahoo! Local. The online guides help people find local businesses, restaurants, retailers and more. In addition, users post reviews of businesses, so ideally your company will receive great word-of-mouth marketing from happy clients. Setting up a business account with Yelp is free, though you can buy sponsorship ads, too. A basic Yahoo! Local Listing is free, and you can upgrade for a small monthly fee." It is smart to consider ways to advertise online, especially nowadays, because people are more likely to research a company, service, or product online instead of through the yellow pages or by word of mouth.

Set up a website for the company. That way, people can research your products and find a place where they can read about it. Setting up a website can cost little to no money. Making it look good can all depend on a free layout on Wordpress, Blogger, or any hosting websites. You can fiddle around with the website, post updates, and give your business a sense that it is relatable. It can also be used as a way of keeping customers aware of new upcoming products and services. Moreover, it will allow for a direct line of communication with customers, which can lead to satisfaction for the customers and then more advertisement through word of mouth and social networking sites.

This leads me to social networking sites. Having a Twitter account will allow you to tweet updates, changes, and announcements in a quick, effortless, and freeway. A Facebook page would allow people to follow any updates as well. You can keep in touch with customers that way as well.

Another piece of advice is to "Submit press releases to local newspapers and business magazines. Be sure the story is newsworthy, not simply an advertisement. Send press releases when you hire new employees, open a branch, win an award, reach a milestone, host an open house, partner with another company, expand your products or services, restructure your business, work with a charity or rebrand your business."

And finally, "Try out cross-promotion. Talk to a non-competing company in your industry about cross promoting your products and services. You could add links to your websites, share a booth at a local trade show or split the costs for a direct mail piece. Many kinds of companies could team up: a hair salon and a clothing boutique, a print shop and a computer repair store, a day care center and a pediatrician, etc." Collaborating with other businesses, sharing business cards, featuring links of each other's sites would allow for more exposure to your business.

Advertising is very important for a business, particularly one that is just starting out, so remember that as you approach other businesses to help you spread the word.

Web advertising

If you run a small business, advertising costs must be figured in as part of your overall expenses. If you have received quotes for phone directory ads, business association block ads, and mostly any other print media, these costs are quite high. So, what if your budget is small, perhaps negligible? Will you be left outside of the advertising arena or are there other avenues to help you get the word out? The answer in one word is: yes. Let's explore ways you can "get the word out" through online means…yes, via the internet!

The rise of the internet has spawned an entire industry with it. You may remember in the late 1990s stories of dot.com companies who made a fortune and then went bust. The "irrational exuberance" of that era has, thankfully, passed by and in its place is a much more rational, but very lively market.

Today's biggest players online are search engine providers led by Google, Yahoo!, and Bing. Between them, these three search engines dominate the market. Mostly everyone today searches the internet for products sold by small businesses to large corporations and these are the people you want to target. Indeed, while Christmas season sales typically increase around 4% year over year for "brick and mortar" retailers, the internet has been seeing year over year increases of 30% and higher! No small business operator should exclude the internet when crafting a marketing plan.

By selecting the advertising plan that works for you, you can have your ads appear on web sites in your local area or across the world and be charged a small amount per click. In other words, you don't pay for advertising unless someone clicks on your ad and goes through to your site. To keep clicks from getting out of control you determine the price per click and the amount per day, week, or month you are willing to pay. No busting of your small business budget!

Banner or text ads on select sites can also be helpful for your small business. If there is a web site you like and you suspect that a lot of your customers would frequent that site, contact the webmaster to learn what his advertising charges would be. Perhaps in exchange for submitting a few helpful articles, the webmaster would waive your advertising fee altogether. Or, at the very least, accept any other help you could provide [moderating a forum, answering questions, etc.].

Another way of getting the word out is through your own web site. No, you don't need a web professional to establish your site, but it does help to have someone who can guide you through the set-up process. At the very least a few pages are what you will need, so set up costs shouldn't be terribly expensive. In addition, figure on paying monthly hosting and domain name fees but these expenses should be no more than $100-$125 per year. Pay a little extra for a web professional who can help you optimize your site [make it search engine friendly] and you'll get your money back much quicker. Finally, check with your accountant for small business tax deductions.

Select the marketing plan that works best for your small business. A mixture of all four points is a great plan of attack for many small business owners…just like you!

Internet marketing…define your mark

When doing internet marketing for small business, you must run an even tighter and more planned campaign than if you were doing it for a large business. The smaller the business, it seems, the more tightly the plan should be. Large companies have a much larger advertising budget, so even if their online marketing strategies aren't very successful, traditional advertising can make a huge difference for them.

But smaller businesses typically don't have thousands of dollars to spend on the more common forms of advertising. Online marketing often becomes the main thrust of the marketing campaign, so it's necessary that it's done very well.

An advantage that small businesses can have over large corporations when it comes to marketing online is that they're more likely to have a very focused niche. While large companies have niches, too, sometimes larger companies market a variety of products and services over a very broad customer base. Then marketing each individual niche must be a separate campaign.

When internet marketing for small business, you'll probably only have to worry about one very specific niche. You'll know exactly what your customers are looking for and can focus on filling that need with every aspect of your marketing plan, instead of having to spread the campaign over several different groups of consumers.

Internet marketing for small business, because of the smaller budgets, often doesn't involve heavy pay-per-click advertising. The cost involved with PPC ads can end up being quite high with not necessarily a very big return. If you have a specific budget set up for PPC marketing, then by all mean use it, but monitor the returns very carefully so you can abandon keywords that aren't working and focus on those that bring in the customers.

Search engine optimization is an excellent method of internet marketing for small business. There can be expense involved if you pay a marketing expert or an SEO service to handle this branch of your marketing efforts, but the money spent will probably be well worth it. This is also where many small businesses fail.

They don't make sure their content is optimized for the search engines, so it's very difficult for someone to find them unless they're searching on the company name. People search for what they want, though, not the company that might have what they're looking for. So internet marketing for small business should always include a plan to get your website higher in the search engine rankings on the best keywords for your company.

Part of the search engine efforts should involve getting other websites to link to yours. Search engines don't just take keywords into account, but they also pay attention to a website's popularity with other sites. The more sites that link to yours, the more valuable your information is according to most search engines. These methods of internet marketing for small business can get a small company's website ranked well ahead of a corporation's, all while spending much less money on advertising.

Chapter 8 Operations
Ways a small business can benefit from a virtual assistant

Hiring a Virtual Assistant (VA) can be one of the smartest businesses moves you will ever make. A good VA will be able to assist you in handling your administrative workload, allowing you more time to focus on growing your business and generating revenue. Here are just ten of many ways that a Virtual Assistant can provide much-needed support to your small business:

1. **General Administrative Support**

    If you ever wished you had an administrative assistant on call, a Virtual Assistant may be the perfect solution for you! VAs can provide general administrative services such as word processing, data entry, spreadsheet and database maintenance, desktop publishing- the list goes on and on. In fact, if you could give it to an administrative assistant, you can give it to a Virtual Assistant!

2. Invoicing

A Virtual Assistant can facilitate your invoicing, ensuring that your clients receive timely, accurate invoices. By partnering with a VA to prepare your invoices, you can gain a tremendous amount of time each month to focus on other aspects of your business that require your specialized attention.

3. Email and Voicemail Management

If you get large numbers of emails or voicemails, a Virtual Assistant can manage your inboxes. They can sort through the spam and reply to messages that don't require your attention, leaving you with fewer messages to wade through every day. A VA can also provide you with a consolidated report of voicemail messages, allowing you to return several important phone calls from a single report.

4. **Online Marketing Management**

A Virtual Assistant can assist you with your online marketing plan. They can manage your pay-per-click campaigns, post articles, submit your website to search engines, add your website to online directories, create banner ads, prepare and send email newsletters, etc. Since VAs make their livings online, many of them keep abreast of the latest trends in online marketing.

5. **Customer Response**

Use a Virtual Assistant's services to keep existing and potential customers happy and returning. A VA can effectively and efficiently handle customer questions and complaints in an appropriate manner. By providing your customers with a timely, helpful response, a VA can help you build a stronger relationship with your customers.

6. **Event Planning**

   Nothing is better than a well-planned event. Enlisting the help of a Virtual Assistant in coordinating your seminars and company functions can take a tremendous amount of burden off your shoulders, allowing for stress-free coordination of your events. They can decide for the location, speakers, catering, photography, etc.- and notify the attendees, too.

7. **Internet Research**

   A Virtual Assistant can efficiently perform internet research, consolidating the information you seek and saving you both time and money. A VA can use their extensive research skills to your benefit, providing you with incredible value by investigating requested topics and providing the results in the desired format.

8. **Calendar Management**

Managing a busy schedule effectively doesn't happen by chance. Team with a Virtual Assistant to help you stay atop of important dates, appointments, contacts, and events. They can help you stay organized and prepared each day, with minimal effort on your part, reminding you of obligations and events ahead of time.

9. **Project Management**

Large and small projects alike can be managed by a Virtual Assistant. A VA can keep your project on track by organizing and coordinating resources, objectives, deliverables, etc. They can relieve the everyday stress of project management while ensuring that deadlines are met, and progress continues.

Guide to small business factoring

Factoring is becoming a popular yet not so well-known tool in the arena of small business. It is an important way of keeping cash flowing through the business when invoices are delayed, or accounts receivable are higher than the money in hand. **Essentially, factoring helps you get cash for your business without having that time delay from the time you issue an invoice**. They also provide you with collection services and sales ledgers that can be helpful as well. If you are a small business owner, then you should consider this guide to small business factoring to fund your business month to month.

How does factoring work? It is easy and yet complicated all at the same time. The factor will generally manage your sales ledger for you while also providing you with collection services for all outstanding invoices. Typically, you will be loaned 80% to 90% of the total amount of the invoice. You will generally receive the money within 24 hours of agreeing to the services of the factor.

Factoring for a small business does cost money, though. Usually there are a couple of different costs you must consider. A service charge will usually cover the management of your sales and collections. The other charge is a percentage of sales factored as well as an interest charge of some sort on the cash advance the factor is giving you. The interest rates, obviously, will depend on your company's credit, the credit of the invoiced companies, and the institution you factor through.

No guide to small business factoring would be complete without telling you want to look for in a factoring company. Obviously, you should look for a stable financial institution that will be able to support the business. You should also look for good terms and a company you are comfortable working with since there will be plenty of interaction. Finally, you may want to consider a company that will give you internet access to your accounts. You can easily track the ledger, sales, collections, and your factored amounts that way.

It is also important to understand that no two factoring companies are completely alike. While much of what this guide to small business factoring has explained is typical, there are exceptions to most every situation. The best thing you can do for your business with regards to factoring is research the companies you are considering. Think about what you need and what you want and what everyone is offering you.

A guide to small business factoring can never be complete. There are too many ins and outs when it comes to almost any financial transaction. There are also several variables involved like current interest rates, your credit rating, reliability of your invoiced companies, and many other things as well.

Before you ever agree to a factoring relationship, make sure you understand all terms as well as how long the contract is for and what renewal terms are. Protect yourself and do your homework and you can use factoring to keep your cash flowing.

www.ingramcontent.com/pod-product-compliance
Lightning Source LLC
Chambersburg PA
CBHW071516220526
45472CB00003B/1049